Knitted Aliens

Fiona McDonald

Search Press

First published in Great Britain 2010

Search Press Limited
Wellwood, North Farm Road,
Tunbridge Wells, Kent TN2 3DR

Text copyright © Fiona McDonald 2010

Photographs by Debbie Patterson at
Search Press Studios

Photographs and design copyright
© Search Press Ltd 2010

ISBN: 978-1-84448-536-9

Suppliers
If you have difficulty in obtaining any of the
materials and equipment mentioned in this book,
then please visit the Search Press website for
details of suppliers: www.searchpress.com

Printed in Malaysia

Abbreviations

beg: beginning

dec: decrease (by working two
stitches together)

g st: garter stitch (knit every row)

inc: increase (by working into the front and
back of the stitch)

k: knit

k2tog: knit two stitches together

p: purl

p2tog: purl two stitches together

rib: ribbing (one stitch knit, one stitch purl)

st(s): stitch(es)

st st: stocking stitch (one row knit, one
row purl)

Contents

Introduction

They have landed and we have made contact at last! Alien lifeforms from distant planets have come to Earth to make new friends and learn about humans.

In this book you will find examples of the inhabitants of many different planets and how to make them. There is also a variation for each one – just as on Earth, where we have different types of a single species, so it is on most other planets. The life forms offered here are but a few of the myriad living organisms found throughout the universe and I am sure it is possible to find many more.

In your quest to depict our visitors do not hesitate to experiment with different colours and textures of yarn. You may like to add beads, sequins and other glittery stuff or swap around different body parts to get even stranger and more beautiful aliens. Your imagination can have full rein.

Above all else, I hope you enjoy making these miniature beings. Now, let's explore the galaxy!

Materials and techniques

Materials

For most of the aliens in this book I have used an 8-ply pure wool called Cleckheaton Country. I have also gathered inexpensive fancy yarns over time and raided my store of these to help the creatures look cute and interesting. If you cannot find the exact same yarn do not be afraid to substitute something else; these are not garments that need precise tension.

I use 3mm needles (UK 11; US 2) for nearly all the work in 8-ply. This is because toys are better with a tighter fabric. However, if you have difficulty managing on these needles, try a larger size.

Many of these aliens are stuffed with polyester fibrefill. This is available as toy stuffing but I use inexpensive pillows. An old slim paintbrush is fantastically useful for getting the stuffing into small places: the bristles help hold the stuffing while it is being positioned. A chopstick is a cheap and useful alternative.

Techniques

You will need a tapestry needle for sewing up seams and an ordinary needle and thread for sewing on bead eyes. I usually sew larger pieces of knitting (such as the main bodies) with the right sides of the seam together, but for small pieces, like arms and legs, I do mattress stitch with the right sides out as it is difficult to turn small pieces right side out once they are sewn up.

Safety

I have not designed these toys for children under three years of age as they have small parts that could be a choking hazard. You can adapt any of the patterns by leaving off small parts like antennae and embroidering the eyes instead of using beads. Make sure you stitch arms and legs on very firmly.

Antennae and tentacles

Antennae:

With a 3mm crochet hook, crochet 7 chain stitch and cut a long thread. Thread this on to a tapestry needle and weave back through crocheted chain and insert into head of alien, secure with a couple of stitches, neaten thread and clip.

You can get exactly the same effect as a crocheted chain by casting on 1 stitch and knitting it, turning it and knitting it again. It is knitting a row of 1 until you reach the desired length. For 7 chain stitch of crochet, knit 7 rows of 1 stitch.

Tentacles:

On 3 mm knitting needles cast on and k1; inc into this [2 sts], then work in stocking stitch until the work reaches the desired length and p2tog. Cast off. Thread the tail of yarn on to a tapestry needle and weave it back through tentacle. This gives it a bit more body.

You can shape the tentacle into a curve by pulling slightly on it. If enough thread is left over, you can use it to secure the tentacle to your alien.

Fragmolite

Materials:

3 balls 8-ply – 1 turquoise, 1 yellow and 1 brown

Small amount of multicoloured fluffy yarn

2 beads for eyes

Polyester fibrefill

Tapestry needle

Sewing needle and thread

Needles:

1 pair 3mm (UK 11; US 2) knitting needles

Instructions:

Body (make 1)

Cast on 20 sts in turquoise.

Rows 1–5: st st.

Rows 6–10: Change to fluffy yarn. Continue in g st.

Rows 11–18: Change back to 8-ply yarn. Continue in st st and cast off.

Head (make 1)

Using 8-ply yarn, cast on 3 sts.

Row 1: inc in each st [6 sts].

Row 2: purl.

Row 3: inc in each st [12 sts].

Row 4: purl.

Row 5: inc each st [24 sts].

Rows 6–16: st st.

Row 17: *k3, inc 1* rep from * to * to end [30 sts].

Rows 18–20: st st.

Row 21: k6.

Rows 22–32: Turn and work on 6 st only in st st.

Row 33: k2tog each end [4 sts].

Row 34: purl.

Row 35: k2tog twice and cast off.

Repeat this pattern on each of the 4 sets of 6 stitches to get 5 tentacles in all.

Arms (make 2)

Cast on 3 sts in brown.

Row 1: inc each st [6 sts].

Rows 2–16: st st.

Row 17: k2tog each end [4 sts].

Row 18: purl.

Row 19: k2tog twice and cast off.

Legs (make 2)

Cast on 3 sts using yellow.

Row 1: inc each st [6 sts].

Rows 2–6: st st.

Rows 7–8: Change colour on knit row to brown and knit 1 row. Purl one row in same colour.

Rows 9–10: Change colour on knit row to yellow and knit 1 row. Purl one row in same colour.

Rows 11–18: Swap colour on next knit row and repeat sequence until you have 3 contrasting stripes (excluding the foot).

Rows 19–24: st st. Cast off on last purl row.

Making up

Fold body in half and secure the centre back seam and bottom seam with mattress stitch (make sure side seam is back seam): Stuff with polyester fibrefill and sew the top shut. Fold each tentacle in half and mattress stitch along the length of the tentacle. Sew the centre back head seam up. Run thread around the opening under the head and gather it together. Stitch the head to body (see inset). Mattress stitch along the arm and leg seams. The limbs do not need to be stuffed. Attach the legs at the base of the body and the arms at the shoulders.

The ocean world of Curcon is covered with placid, methane-rich seas, which the peace-loving Fragmolites love to explore.

Pssscattlin

Materials:

2 balls 8-ply – 1 white and 1 red

1 ball of black fluffy yarn

Small amount of pink 8-ply yarn for mouth

2 beads for eyes

Polyester fibrefill

Tapestry needle

Sewing needle and thread

2 pipe cleaners for legs

Needles:

1 pair 3mm (UK 11; US 2) knitting needles

Instructions:

Body (make 2)

Cast on 4 sts in black fluffy thread.
Row 1: inc each stitch [8 sts].
Row 2: purl.
Row 3: inc each stitch [16 sts].
Row 4: purl.
Row 5: inc 1 each end of knit row [18 sts].
Row 6: purl.
Row 7: inc 1 each end of knit row [20 sts].
Rows 8–22: st st.
Row 23: k8, cast off 6, k to end.
Rows 24–34: Turn. Working on the 7 sts from row 23 only: st st.
Row 35: k2tog each end of k row [5 sts].
Row 36: purl.
Row 37: k2tog each end [3 sts].
Row 38: purl and cast off.
Return to remaining 7 sts and repeat for second ear.

Face (make 1)

Cast on 3 sts in white.
Row 1: inc each st [6 sts].
Row 2: purl.
Row 3: inc each st [12 sts].
Rows 4–6: st st.
Row 7: k5, inc in each of next 2 sts, k5 [14 sts].
Rows 8–10: st st.
Row 11: k5, k2tog twice, k5 [12 sts].
Rows 12–14: st st.
Row 15: k2tog along row [6 sts].

Row 16: purl.
Row 17: k2tog along row [3 sts].
Row 18: purl and cast off.

Legs (make 4)

Cast on 6 stitches in white.
Row 1: inc every stitch [12 sts].
Row 2: purl.
Row 3: inc each stitch [24 sts].
Row 4: purl.
Row 5: k2tog along row [12 sts].
Row 6: purl.
Row 7: k2tog along row [6 sts].
Row 8: purl.
Rows 9–10: bring in red and knit a row followed by a purl row. Alternate between white and red on each knit row for stripes.
Rows 11–30: repeat rows 9 and 10, ten times.

Tail (make 1)

Cast on 3 in white.
Row 1: inc each stitch [6 sts].
Rows 2–6: st st.
Rows 7–8: bring in red on row 7, knit row and proceed as for the leg stripes until desired tail length is reached (it can be as long or short as you like).

Making up

Stitch the bodies together using mattress stitch, leaving an opening at the bottom. Stuff it firmly and stitch it shut. Pin the face to the centre of the front body. Mattress stitch it on to the body, stuffing it as you go until it is firmly stuffed and stitched on. Needlesculpt the nose using the tapestry needle and white yarn: push the needle in at the edge of the face leaving the thread hanging out (to be removed later). Bring the needle out at one side of the nose bump. Take a small stitch and push it through to the other side of the nose. Repeat back and forth a couple of times until the nose is shaped.

Push the thread through to the edge of the face and snip it off. Sew bead eyes on to either side of the nose. Make two antennae (see page 7) and stitch them in place. Sew the legs up from the outside. Insert a pipe cleaner through the base of the body and pull it out 2cm (¾in) away and insert it where legs should be. Push the knitted legs on to the pipe cleaner, bend and twist the pipe cleaner to the correct length, then sew the legs to the body around where the pipe cleaner enters the body.

Repeat for the other pair of legs, then sew the tail on from the outside and stitch to the figure's back.

Pssscattlins are prairie-roaming aliens from the dust world of Querepole. The curious inhabitants spend all day running from horizon to horizon, searching for new things to see and do.

11

Narle

Materials:

3 balls 8-ply – 1 aqua, 1 yellow and 1 cream

Small amounts of pink and brown 8-ply yarn for mouth and eyebrows

2 beads for eyes

Polyester fibrefill

Tapestry needle

Sewing needle and pink thread

Needles:

1 pair 3mm (UK 11; US 2) knitting needles

Instructions:

Body (make 2)

Cast on 10sts in aqua.

Rows 1–2: g st.

Rows 3–4: bring in yellow; knit row followed by a purl row.

Rows 5–6: repeat rows 3–4.

Rows 7–8: change colour to aqua and g st.

Rows 9–12: change colour to yellow and st st.

Row 13: change colour to aqua and knit row.

Row 14: k2tog each end [8 sts].

Rows 15–16: change colour to yellow and g st.

Row 17: k2tog each end [6 sts].

Rows 18–19: change colour to aqua and g st.

Row 20 (tail): change colour to yellow, k1 inc. each end [8 sts].

Row 21: purl.

Row 22: k inc 1 at beg row, p2, k2, p2, k inc last st [10 sts].

Row 23: p2, k2, p2, k2, p2; k inc first st, p3, k2, p3, k inc last st [12 sts].

Row 24: k1, p2, k2, p1.

Turn and work on these 6 sts only.

Row 25: k1, p3, k1; p3, k2, p1; k2tog, k4; p3, p2tog.

Row 26: knit and cast off.

Rejoin other side and work as follows:

Row 1: p1, k2, p2, k1.

Row 2: k2, p3, k1.

Row 3: p1, k2, p3.

Row 4: k4, k2tog.

Row 5: p2tog, p3.

Row 6: knit and cast off.

Face (make 1)

Cast on 3 in cream.

Row 1: inc each st [6 sts].

Row 2: purl.

Row 3: inc each st [12 sts].

Rows 4–6: st st.

Row 7: shape ears – cast on 2 sts at beg of row then k6, k inc in next 2, k6 [16 sts].

Row 8: cast on 2 sts at beg of p row, p to end [18 sts].

Rows 9–10: st st.

Row 11: cast off 2 sts at beg of row, k4, k2tog twice, k to end [14 sts].

Row 12: cast off 2 sts at beg of p row, p to end [12 sts].

Rows 13–14: st st.

Row 15: k2tog along row [6 sts].

Row 16: purl.

Row 17: k2tog along row [3 sts].

Row 18: purl and cast off.

Arms (make 2)

Cast on 12 sts in cream.

Rows 1–4: st st.

Row 5: k2tog along row [6 sts].

Rows 6–20: st st.

Row 21: k2tog along row [3 sts].

Row 22: purl and cast off.

Fin (make 1)

Cast on 10 sts in aqua.

Row 1: inc each st [20 sts].

Row 2: purl.

Row 3: inc each st [40 sts].

Row 4: k1, p1 rep to end of row.

Rows 5–6: repeat row 4 twice more.

Row 7: purl, then cast off.

Making up

Sew the body up, right sides together, leaving the head end open. Lightly stuff the body and pin the face into the opening, leaving the ears free. Stitch the opening closed. Fold the arms in half lengthwise with wrong sides together and mattress stitch them shut. Stitch the arms to the body just behind the face. Stitch the body on either side of face. Sew the fin along the back of the body.

Needlesculpt the nose using the tapestry needle and cream yarn, then sew on beads for eyes using a tapestry needle and thread. To finish, use pink yarn for the mouth, and brown yarn for the eyebrows.

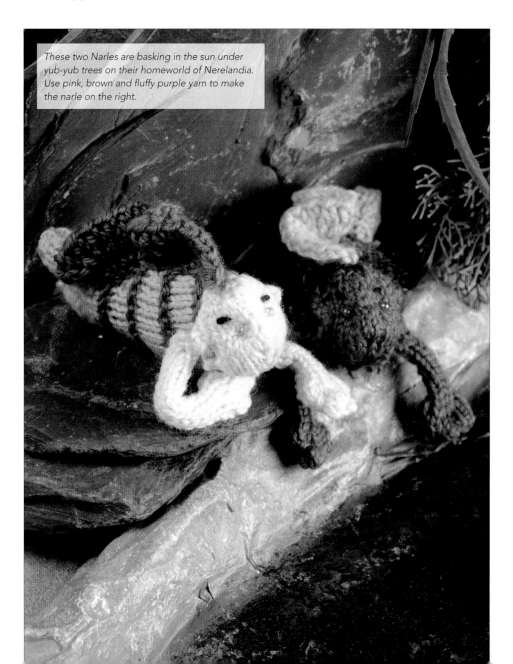

These two Narles are basking in the sun under yub-yub trees on their homeworld of Nerelandia. Use pink, brown and fluffy purple yarn to make the narle on the right.

Rasteroni

Materials:

2 balls 8-ply – 1 aqua and 1 turquoise

Small amount of blue 8-ply yarn for antennae

2 beads and small amount of white felt for eyes

Polyester fibrefill

Tapestry needle

Sewing needle and black thread

Pipe cleaner

Needles:

1 pair 3mm (UK 11; US 2) knitting needles

Instructions:

Body (make 1)

Cast on 8 sts in aqua.
Row 1: inc each st [16 sts].
Row 2: purl.
Row 3: inc every 2nd stitch [24 sts].
Row 4: purl.
Row 5: inc 1st each end [26 sts].
Rows 6–24: st st.
Row 25: k2tog row [13 sts].
Row 26: purl.
Row 27: k2tog three times, k1, k2tog three times [7 sts].
Rows 28–38: st st.
Row 39: k2tog each end [5 sts].
Row 40: purl.
Row 41: k2tog each end [3 sts].
Row 42: purl and cast off.

Neck (make 1)

Cast on 10 sts in turquoise
Rows 1–13: st st.
Row 14: purl and cast off.

Head (make 1)

cast on 3 in turquoise.
Row 1: inc each st [6 sts].
Row 2: purl.
Row 3: inc each st [12 sts].
Row 4: purl.
Row 5: inc 1 each end [14 sts].
Row 6: purl.

Row 7: inc 1 each end [16 sts].
Row 8: purl. Bring in aqua.
Rows 9–22: st st; change colours every knit row to get striped effect.
Row 23: change back to aqua and knit row.
Row 24: p2tog each end [14 sts].
Row 25: knit.
Row 26: p2tog each end [12 sts].
Row 27: k row; p2tog along row [6 sts].
Row 28: knit.
Row 29: p2tog along row [3 sts].
Row 30: knit and cast off.

Flippers (make 2)

Cast on 20 sts in aqua.
Rows 1–2: st st.
Row 3: k2tog each end [18 sts].
Row 4: purl.
Row 5: k2tog each end [16 sts].
Row 6: purl.
Row 7: k2tog each end [14 sts].
Row 8: purl.
Row 9: k2tog each end [12 sts].
Row 10: purl.
Row 11: k2tog each end [10 sts].
Row 12: purl.
Row 13: k2tog each end [8 sts].
Row 14: purl.
Row 15: k2tog each end [6 sts].
Row 16: purl.
Row 17: k2tog each end [4 sts].
Row 18: purl.
Row 19: k2tog and cast off.

Making up

Fold the body in half, right sides together. Using aqua yarn, stitch from the tail to the neck opening, turn right side out and stuff. Fold the neck in half lengthwise, wrong sides together, and stitch up the length, sewing one end to the neck opening on the body. For a stiffer neck, insert a pipe cleaner into the body and neck. Stuff the neck around the pipe cleaner. Fold the head lengthwise, right sides together, and sew the seam from each far end of the head. Leave an opening in the middle of the head where the neck should go. Turn the head right side out and fill with stuffing. Place the head opening on the neck opening and sew. Fold the flippers in half, right sides together, and sew from point to larger end. Turn right side out, but do not stuff. Squash flipper flat so seam is in the centre and sew on to the side of the body with seam facing down. Repeat for the other side. Make two antennae (see page 7) from blue yarn and cut two slivers of white felt to glue under beads for eyes.

Rasteroni are lighter than air, and enjoy drifting through the multicoloured gas clouds of the Blip nebula.

Bilk

Materials:

2 balls 8-ply – 1 terracotta and 1 turquoise

2 beads and small amount of white felt for eyes and mouth

Polyester fibrefill

Tapestry needle

Sewing needle and black thread

Permanent black marker pen

Needles:

1 pair 3mm (UK 11; US 2) knitting needles

Instructions:

Body (make 1)

Cast on 10 sts in terracotta.
Row 1: inc each st [20 sts].
Row 2: purl.
Row 3: inc 1 each end [22 sts].
Row 4: purl.
Row 5: inc 1 each end [24 sts].
Rows 6–10: st st.
Row 11: *k1, k inc 1* repeat from * to * to end [36 sts].
Rows 12–20: st st.
Row 21: k1, k2tog along row [24 sts].
Row 22: purl.
Row 23: k2tog along row [12 sts].
Rows 24–28: st st.
Row 29: *k1 k inc 1* repeat from * to* to end [18 sts].
Row 30: purl.
Row 31: k9, cast off 2, k to end. Turn and work on these 8 sts only.
Row 32: p inc 1 each end [10 sts].
Row 33: k inc 1 each end [12 sts].
Row 34: p inc 1 each end [14 sts].
Row 35: k inc 1 each end [16 sts].
Rows 34–38: st st.
Row 39: k2tog along row [8 sts].
Row 40: purl.
Row 41: k2tog along row [4 sts].
Row 42: p2tog and cast off. Repeat these rows on other eyestalk.

Legs (make 2)

Cast on 3 sts in terracotta.
Row 1: inc each st [6 sts].
Row 2: purl.
Row 3: inc each st [12 sts].
Row 4: purl.
Row 5: inc each st [24 sts].
Row 6: purl. Change to terracotta.
Rows 7–8: st st. Change to turquoise.
Rows 9–10: st st. Change to terracotta.
Rows 11–12: st st.
Cast off on last p row.

Arms (make 2)

Cast on 3 sts in terracotta.
Row 1: inc each st [6 sts].
Row 2: purl.
Row 3: inc each st [12 sts].
Row 4: purl. Bring in turquoise.
Rows 5–6: st st. Change to terracotta.
Rows 7–8: st st. Change to turquoise.
Row 9: st st. Cast off on last p row.

Making up

Fold the body in half, right sides together, and mattress stitch it closed, leaving it open at the neck where the eyestalks divide. Turn it right-side out and stuff the body. Fold each eyestalk in half and mattress stitch down from the top. Stuff each eyestalk and stitch the opening shut after stuffing the neck area.

Sew each arm and leg up the side seams, with wrong sides facing. Stuff and stitch the limbs to the body. Cut two little almonds of white felt and glue in eye area. Sew bead over each. Cut a larger almond from white felt and glue it to the mouth area. Use a fine permanent marker to draw in lines for teeth.

Bilks are exceptionally nosey creatures from Kornoble, so being able to see in two directions at once is very useful! The green Bilk is made with aqua, turquoise and green yarn. Some pink felt was cut into the shape of lips and glued on before the mouth.

Zurk

Materials:

4 balls 8-ply – 1 brown, 1 pink, 1 purple and 1 lilac

2 beads for eyes

Small amount of blue felt and blue yarn for mouth and nostrils

Polyester fibrefill

Tapestry needle

Sewing needle and black thread

Needles:

1 pair 3mm (UK 11; US 2) knitting needles

Instructions:

Body/head (make 1)

Cast on 6 sts in brown.
Row 1: inc each st [12 sts].
Row 2: purl.
Row 3: inc each st [24 sts].
Rows 4: purl.
Rows 5–14: st st.
Row 15: *k1 inc 1* repeat from * to * to end of row [36 sts].
Rows 16–32: st st.
Row 33: k1, k2tog along row [24 sts].
Row 34: purl.
Row 35: k2tog along row [12 sts].
Row 36: purl.
Row 37: k2tog along row [6 sts].
Row 38: p2tog three times. Cast off.

Mouth (make 1)

Cast on 5 sts in lilac.
Row 1: inc each st [10 sts].
Row 2: purl.
Row 3: inc each st [20 sts].
Rows 4–8: st st.
Row 9: k2tog along row [10 sts].
Row 10: purl.
Row 11: k2tog along row [5 sts].
Row 12: purl and cast off.

Legs (make 2)

Cast on 3 sts in purple.
Row 1: inc each st [6 sts].
Row 2: purl. Bring in pink.

Rows 3–4: st st. Change to purple.
Rows 5–6: st st. Change to pink.
Rows 7–8: st st. Change to purple.
Rows 9–10: st st. Change to pink.
Rows 11–12: st st. Change to purple.
Rows 13–14: st st. Change to pink.
Rows 15–16: st st. Change to purple.
Rows 17–18: st st. Change to pink.
Rows 19–20: st st. Change to purple.
Rows 21–22: st st. Change to pink.
Rows 23–24: st st. Change to purple.
Rows 25–26: st st. Change to pink.
Rows 27–28: st st. Change to purple.
Rows 29–30: st st; cast off on last p row.

Arms (make 2)

Cast on 2 in purple.
Row 1: inc each st [4 sts].
Row 2: purl. Bring in pink.
Rows 3–4: st st. Change to purple.
Rows 5–6: st st. Change to pink.
Rows 7–8: st st. Change to purple.
Rows 9–10: st st. Change to pink.
Rows 11–12: st st. Change to purple.
Rows 13–14: st st. Change to pink.
Rows 15–16: st st. Change to purple.
Row 17: p2tog twice and cast off.

Making up

Fold the body/head piece in half lengthways with the right sides together. Back stitch along the centre back seam, leaving an opening at the bottom for stuffing. Turn it the right side out and stuff firmly. Stitch the opening closed. Pin the mouth section about a third of the way up the body, then mattress stitch it to the body, stuffing as you go. Cut a lip-shaped piece of blue felt and sew it to the mouth section. With a length of blue yarn, stitch across from one side of the mouth to the other and pull firmly to sculpt. Stitch two nostrils on the mouth section using blue yarn. Sew on beads for eyes. Make six tentacles (see page 7) and sew three on either side of the head. Make two antennae (see page 7) and stitch above the eyes. Turn the arms and legs right sides out and use mattress stitch to stitch them up. Sew the legs to the bottom of the torso and the two arms on either side of the body just below the mouth.

The wise and enigmatic Zurks spend their long lives stargazing and contemplating the mysteries of the universe from their home planet of Abzed. Their many head tentacles pick up signals from the cosmos, and allow them to communicate telepathically. Try using fluffy wool for a Zurk in their winter pelt.

Pilquat

Materials:

2 balls 8-ply – 1 cream and 1 pink

1 ball multicoloured fluffy yarn

2 beads for eyes

Small amount of red felt for mouth

Polyester fibrefill

Tapestry needle

Sewing needle and black thread

Needles:

1 pair 3mm (UK 11; US 2) knitting needles

Instructions:

Body (make 1)
Cast on 48 sts in multicoloured fluffy yarn.
Rows 1–7: st st.
Row 8: k2tog along row [24 sts].
Row 9: knit.
Row 10: k2tog along row [12 sts].
Row 11: knit.
Row 12: k2tog along row [6 sts].
Row 13: knit.
Row 14: k2tog along row [3 sts].
Row 15: purl. Cast off.

Head (make 1)
Cast on 24 sts in cream.
Rows 1–10: st st.
Row 11: k11, k inc in each of 2 next sts, k11 [26 sts].
Row 12: purl.
Row 13: k11, k2tog twice, k11 [24 sts].
Row 14: purl.
Row 15: k2tog along row [12 sts].
Row 16: purl.
Row 17: k2tog along row [6 sts].
Row 18: purl.
Row 19: k2tog along row [3 sts] and cast off.

Ears (make 2)
Cast on 4 sts in cream.
Rows 1–2: st st.
Row 3: k2tog [2 sts].
Row 4: p2tog cast off.

Legs (make 2)
Cast on 3 sts in pink.
Row 1: inc each st [6 sts].
Row 2: purl. Bring in cream.
Rows 3–4: st st. Change to pink.
Rows 5–6: st st. Change to cream.
Rows 7–8: st st. Change to pink.
Rows 9–10: st st. Change to cream.
Rows 11–12: st st. Change to pink.
Rows 13–14: st st. Change to cream.
Rows 15–16: st st. Change to pink.
Rows 17–18: st st. Change to cream.
Rows 19–20: st st. Change to pink.
Rows 21–22: st st. Change to cream.
Rows 23–24: st st. Change to pink.
Rows 25–26: st st. Change to cream.
Rows 27–28: st st. Cast off.

Arms (make 2)
Cast on 2 in cream.
Row 1: inc each st [4 sts].
Rows 2–17: st st.
Row 18: p2tog and cast off.

Making up

Sew up the centre back seams of the head and body. Turn each the right side out. Stuff the head and stitch it into the body cup. Needlesculpt the nose with a couple of stitches on either side of the bump.

Sew up the the arms and legs with right sides out and stitch in place. Make two antennae from pink yarn (see page 7) and stitch in place on the head. Finish by sewing on two beads as eyes, and making a little embroidered mouth.

The diminutive Pilquats occupy two worlds. Those from Jellick III are dark in colour, with blue antennae. Jellick IV is covered in shifting ferrous icefields, and Pilquats here are white and pink in colour – all the better to blend in to cause mischief!

Grosperneatt

Materials:

2 balls 8-ply – 1 light brown and 1 cream
1 ball multicoloured fluffy yarn
Small amount of brown yarn for mouth
2 beads for eyes
Polyester fibrefill
Tapestry needle
Sewing needle and black thread

Needles:

1 pair 3mm (UK 11; US 2) knitting needles

Instructions:

Body (make 1):
Cast on 10 sts in light brown.
Row 1: inc each st [20 sts].
Row 2: purl.
Row 3: inc each st [40 sts].
Rows 4–16: st st.
Row 17: *k1, k2tog* rep from * to * to end.
Rows 18–20: st st.
Row 21: *k1, k2tog* rep from * to * to end.
Row 22: purl. Cast off.

Horns (make 2)
Cast on 3 sts in cream.
Row 1: inc each st [6 sts].
Row 2: purl.
Rows 3–31: st st.
Row 32: k2tog [3 sts].
Row 33: purl. Cast off.

Making up
Fold the body in half with right sides facing. Sew up the centre back seam, leaving the bottom end open. Turn it the right side out, then stuff and stitch closed. Needlesculpt the nose and sew on beads for eyes.

Sew the horns along their whole length, right side out. Position them on the head and stitch in place. Curl horns and stitch them into the desired shape. Make four tentacles (see page 7) from the fluffy yarn and sew them on to the body.

Make two antennae (see page 7) from brown yarn and stitch either side of mouth area.

The Grosperneatt's homeworld of Treen is regularly scoured by hard-driving dust winds, so the inhabitants have long tentacles to anchor themselves to the rocks. Fancy, fluffy wool will help you to create a hill-dwelling highland Grosperneatt.

Jorna

Materials:

2 balls 8-ply – 1 variegated purple and 1 lilac

1 ball multicoloured fluffy yarn

Small amount of red yarn for mouth and aqua yarn for antennae

2 beads for eyes

Polyester fibrefill

Tapestry needle

Sewing needle and black thread

Needles:

1 pair 3mm (UK 11; US 2) knitting needles

Instructions:

Body (make 1)

Cast on 10 sts in variegated purple.
Row 1: inc each st [20 sts].
Row 2: purl.
Row 3: *k1, inc 1* rep from * to * to end [30 sts].
Row 4: purl.
Row 5: k12, k inc in each of next 6 st, k12 [36 sts].
Rows 6–18: st st.
Row 19: k12, k2tog six times, k12 [30 sts].
Row 20: purl.
Row 21: *k1, k2tog* rep from * to * to end [20 sts].
Rows 22–30: st st.
Row 31: k2tog row [10 sts].
Row 32: purl.
Row 33: k2tog row [5 sts].
Row 34: purl and cast off.

Ears (make 2)

Cast on 4 sts in lilac.
Rows 1–2: st st.
Row 3: k2tog [2 sts].
Row 4: p2tog. Cast off.

Face (make 1)

Cast on 2 sts in lilac.
Row 1: inc each st [4 sts].
Row 2: purl.
Rows 3–4: rep rows 1 and 2 once [8 sts].

Row 5: purl.
Row 6: k3, inc next 2 k3 [10 sts].
Row 7: purl.
Row 8: k3, k inc next 4, k3 [14 sts].
Row 9: purl.
Row 10: k3, inc next 8, k3 [22 sts].
Rows 11–13: st st.
Row 14: k2tog each end [20 sts].
Row 15: purl.
Row 16: k2tog, k3, k2tog five times, k3, k2tog [13 sts].
Row 17: purl.
Row 18: k2tog three times, k1, k2tog three times [7 sts].
Row 19: purl.
Row 20: k2tog, k3, k2tog [5 sts].
Row 21: p2tog, p1, p2tog [3 sts]. Cast off.

Making up

Sew up the back up the centre seam, leaving a small opening. Stuff the alien through this opening, then stitch shut. Pin face on to front of body and stitch on, stuffing as you go. Needlesculpt the nose, then sew on beads for eyes. Embroider a simple mouth, then sew on the ears. Finally, make two antennae (see page 7) and stitch in place.

The moons of Selvinia are dotted with exciting caves amongst which the fun-loving Jornae can hide and explore to their heart's content.

Klem

Materials:

3 balls 8-ply – 1 terracotta, 1 light brown and
    1 cream

Small amount of pink yarn for mouth, fluffy
    yarn for ruff and purple yarn for antennae

2 beads for eyes

Polyester fibrefill

Tapestry needle

Sewing needle and black thread

Needles:

1 pair 3mm (UK 11; US 2) knitting needles

Instructions:

Body (make 1)

Cast on 10 sts in terracotta.
Row 1: inc each st [20 sts].
Rows 2–20: st st.
Row 21: k2tog along row [10 sts].
Rows 22–24: st st.
Row 25: inc each st [20 sts].
Row 26: purl.
Row 27: inc 1 each end [22 sts].
Row 28: purl.
Row 29: inc 1 each end [24 sts].
Rows 30–38: st st.
Row 39: k2tog along row [12 sts].
Row 40: purl.
Row 41: k2tog along row [6 sts].
Row 42: purl and cast off.

Tummy panel (make 1)

Cast on 5 sts in light brown.
Row 1: inc each st [10 sts].
Rows 2–5: g st.
Row 6: purl.
Rows 7–11: g st.
Row 12: purl.
Row 13: knit.
Row 14: purl.
Rows 15–17: g st.
Row 18: k2tog along row [5 sts].
Row 19: knit and cast off.

Face (make 1)

Cast on 8 sts in cream.
Row 1: k inc 1 each end [10 sts].
Row 2: p inc 1 each end [12 sts].
Row 3: k inc 1 each end [14 sts].
Row 4: p inc 1 each end [16 sts].
Row 5: k inc 1, k6, k inc in next 2, k6, k inc 1 [20 sts].
Rows 6–8: st st.
Row 9: k8, k2tog twice, k8 [18 sts].
Rows 10–14: st st.
Row 15: k2tog each end [16 sts].
Row 16: p2tog each end [14 sts].
Rows 17: k2tog each end [12 sts].
Row 18: p2tog each end [10 sts].
Row 19: k2tog each end [8 sts].
Row 20: purl and cast off.

Arms and legs (make 2 of each)

Cast on 2 in terracotta.
Row 1: inc each st [4 sts].
Rows 2–11: st st.
Row 12: p2tog and cast off.

Ears (make 2)

Cast on 6 in terracotta.
Row 1: knit.
Row 2: purl.
Row 3: k2tog each end [4 sts].
Row 4: purl.
Row 5: k2tog [3 sts].
Row 6: purl and cast off.

Making up

Pin the tummy panel to the body, right sides together, and sew along each side panel seam and across the bottom. Turn the right side out and stuff. Pin the face into the hole in the head and stitch it on, stuffing as you go. Needlesculpt the nose, sew on two beads for eyes, then attach the knitted ears and embroider a mouth with pink yarn. Weave a fancy yarn in and out of the stitches around the face for a fur ruff. Finally, make two purple and one terracotta antennae (see page 7), and attach them as antennae and a tail respectively.

Wisps of stellar gas turn the night sky of Upp into a brilliant display of ghostly greens and blues. The sleepy Klem enjoy stargazing from their ice-bound hilltop homes.

Dimmiple

Materials:

2 balls 8-ply – 1 turquoise and 1 aqua

Small amount of purple yarn for nose

Small amount of white felt for mouth

Polyester fibrefill

Tapestry needle

Sewing needle and black thread

Permanent black marker pen

Needles:

1 pair 3mm (UK 11; US 2) knitting needles

Instructions:

Body (make 1)

Cast on 3 sts in turquoise.
Row 1: inc each st [6 sts].
Row 2: purl.
Row 3: inc each st [12 sts].
Row 4: purl.
Row 5: inc each st [24 sts].
Row 6: purl.
Row 7: *k1, inc 1* rep from * to * to end [36 sts].
Row 8: purl.
Row 9: *k1, inc 1* rep from * to * to end [54 sts].
Rows 10–12: st st. Bring in aqua.
Row 13: *k1, k2tog* rep from * to * to end [36 sts].
Row 14: purl. Change to turquoise.
Row 15: *k1, k2tog* rep from * to * to end [24 sts].
Row 16: purl.
Row 17: k2tog along row [12 sts].
Row 18: purl.
Row 19: k2tog along row [6 sts].
Row 20: purl and cast off.

Eyeballs (make 2)

Cast on 3 sts in turquoise.
Row 1: inc each st [6 sts].
Row 2: purl.

Row 3: inc each st [12 sts].
Row 4: purl.
Row 5: inc each st [24 sts].
Rows 6–8: st st.
Row 9: k2tog along row [12 sts].
Row 10: purl.
Row 11: k2tog along row [6 sts].
Row 12: purl.
Row 13: k2tog along row [3 sts].
Row 14: purl and cast off.

Eyeball stalks (make 2)

Cast on 6 sts in aqua.
Rows 1–7: st st.
Row 8: purl and cast off.

Arms (make 2)

Cast on 2 sts in aqua.
Row 1: inc each st [4 sts].
Rows 2–11: st st.
Row 12: p2tog and cast off.

Legs (make 2)

Cast on 2 sts in aqua.
Row 1: inc each st [4 sts].
Rows 2–14: st st.
Row 15: p2tog and cast off.

Nose (make 1)

Cast on 2 sts in purple,
and follow instructions for the legs (above).

Making up

Sew the body and the two eyeballs up the centre back seams, right side out, leaving an opening for stuffing. Stuff each and stitch them closed. Roll the eyeball stalks up, then stitch along the length to make a short thick column. Stitch each of the stalks to the top of the body, then stitch an eyeball on top of each stalk. Embroider a pupil on to the top of each with aqua yarn. Stitch the arms, legs and nose up the length from the right side. Stitch the legs on under the body and the arms at the side. Stitch the nose on to the body just below the top. Add a felt mouth and draw on teeth with a felt pen.

Dimmiplii are exceptionally annoying little creatures from Taerg that flit around while producing a high-pitched whine. Fortunately, they are very easily distracted by shiny things. Since Dimmiplii periodically change their colour (just like a gobstopper), why not try some unusual yarns?

Materials:

2 balls 8-ply – 1 red and 1 light brown

2 beads for eyes

Polyester fibrefill

Tapestry needle

Sewing needle and black thread

Instructions:

Body (make 1)

Cast on 28 sts in red.

Rows 1–8: g st. Change to light brown.

Rows 9–16: st st.

Row 17: k2tog along row [14 sts].

Row 18: purl.

Row 19: k2tog along row [7 sts].

Row 20: purl.

Row 21: k2tog twice, k1, k2tog twice [4 sts]

Row 22: p2tog, cast off.

Head (make 1):

Cast on 3 sts in light brown.

Row 1: inc each st [6 sts].

Row 2: purl.

Row 3: inc each st [12 sts].

Row 4: purl.

Row 5: *k1, k inc1* rep
from * to * to end [18 sts].

Rows 6–24: st st.

Row 25: *k1, k2 tog* rep from *
to * to end [12 sts].

Row 26: purl.

Row 27: k2tog along row [6 sts].

Row 28: purl.

Row 29: k2tog along row [3 sts].

Row 30: purl and cast off.

Arms (make 2)

Cast on 2 sts in red.

Row 1: inc each st [4 sts].

Rows 2–11: st st.

Row 12: p2tog, cast off.

Legs (make 2)

Cast on 3 sts in red.

Row 1: inc each st [6 sts].

Row 2: purl.

Row 3: inc each st [12 sts].

Needles:

1 pair 3mm (UK 11; US 2) knitting needles

Row 4: purl. Bring in light brown.

Rows 5–6: st st. Change to red.

Rows 7–8: st st. Change to light brown.

Rows 9–10: st st. Cast off on last p row.

Fin (make 1)

Cast on 2 sts in red.

Row 1: inc each st [4 sts].

Next, g st until work measures 16cm (6¼in).

Last row: k2tog and cast off.

Ears (make 2)

Cast on 6 sts in red.

Row 1: knit.

Row 2: purl.

Row 3: bring in light brown and k2tog
each end [4 sts].

Row 4: purl.

Row 5: Change to red and k2tog.

Row 6: purl and cast off.

Making up

Fold the body in half, right sides together, and sew up the centre back seam. Turn it right side out and stuff. Stitch the opening closed. Fold the head in half, right sides together, and sew along from each end, leaving an opening in the middle. Turn the head right side out and stuff. Place the opening over the neck and stitch the pieces together. Needlesculpt the nose. Stitch the arms up back seam, stuff and stitch them to the body, then repeat for the legs. Stitch the fin on down the back of the body and head. Sew the ears on to the head and attach beads for eyes with the needle and thread.

Glong is extremely cold, and Helipops are naturally coloured blue and dreadfully miserable. Fortunately, the planet is pocked with lava pools, where the Helipops gather. As they warm up, they change colour to a cheerful red-orange, and sing in a warbling drone.

Welpmina

Materials:

2 balls 8-ply – 1 turquoise and 1 cream

Small amount of aqua yarn for antennae

2 beads for eyes

Polyester fibrefill

Sewing needle and black thread

Pipe cleaner

Needles:

1 pair 3mm (UK 11; US 2) knitting needles

Instructions:

Body and head (make 1)

Cast on 28 sts in turquoise.

Rows 1–20: st st.

Row 21: k2tog along row [14 sts].

Row 22: purl.

Row 23: k2tog three times, k2, k2 tog three times [8 sts].

Row 24: purl. Bring in cream for neck.

Rows 25–30: st st.

Row 21: k2, k inc next 4 st, k2 [12 sts].

Row 22: purl.

Row 23: k inc each st [24 sts].

Row 24: purl.

Row 25: *k1, k inc* rep from * to * to end [36 sts].

Rows 26–40: st st.

Row 41: k2tog along row [18 sts].

Row 42: purl.

Row 43: k2tog along row [9 sts].

Row 44: p row.

Row 45: k2tog twice, k1, k2tog twice [5 sts].

Row 46: p2tog, p1, p2tog and cast off.

Left ear (make 1)

Cast on 5 sts in cream.

Rows 1–8: st st.

Row 9: k2tog at beg of row, k to end [4 sts].

Row 10: purl.

Row 11: k2tog at beg of row, k to end [4 sts].

Row 12: purl and cast off.

Right ear (make 1)

Cast on 5 sts in cream.

Rows 1–8: st st.

Row 9: k to last 2st, k2tog [4 sts].

Row 10: purl.

Row 11: k to last 2st, k2tog [4 sts].

Row 12: purl and cast off.

Arms (make 2)

Cast on 2 sts in cream.

Row 1: inc each st [4 sts].

Rows 2–31: st st.

Row 32: p2tog and cast off.

Legs (make 2)

Cast on 3 sts in cream.

Row 1: inc each st [6 sts].

Rows 2–41: st st.

Row 42: purl and cast off.

Making up

Fold the body in half, wrong sides together. Stitch up the centre back seam, leaving the back of the neck open to help stuff head. Stuff the head and body. Insert a pipe cleaner into body, up the neck and into the head for a stiffer neck. Sew up the openings. Place the ears on either side of the head and sew them on. Sew the arms and legs in place and make two antennae (see page 7) for the top of the head. Sew on two small beads for eyes.

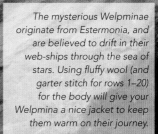

The mysterious Welpminae originate from Estermonia, and are believed to drift in their web-ships through the sea of stars. Using fluffy wool (and garter stitch for rows 1–20) for the body will give your Welpmina a nice jacket to keep them warm on their journey.

Ulgario

Materials:

3 balls 8-ply – 1 turquoise, 1 yellow and 1 brown

1 ball multicoloured fluffy yarn

2 beads for eyes

Polyester fibrefill

Sewing needle and black thread

Needles:

1 pair 3mm (UK 11; US 2) knitting needles

Instructions:

Body (make 1)
Cast on 20 sts in fancy yarn.
Rows 1–5: st st.
Rows 6–10: g st.
Rows 11–21: st st. Cast off on last row.

Head (make 1)
Cast on 3 sts in turquoise.
Row 1: inc each st [6 sts].
Row 2: purl.
Row 3: inc each st [12 sts].
Rows 4–8: st st.
Row 9: k inc each st [24 sts].
Row 10: purl.
Row 11: k8, inc each next 8 st, k8 [32 sts].
Rows 12–16: st st.
Row 17: k2tog along row [16 sts].
Row 18: purl.
Row 19: k2tog along row [8 sts].
Row 20: purl.
Row 21: k2tog along row [4 sts].
Row 22: p2tog and cast off.

Feet (make 2)
Cast on 4 sts in yellow.
Row 1: inc each st [8 sts].
Row 2: purl.
Row 3: k inc 1 each end [10 sts].
Rows 4–8: st st.
Row 9: cast off 2 st at beg of row, k to end [8 sts].
Row 10: p, cast off 2 at beg of row and p to end [6 sts].
Row 11: cast off 2 st at beg of row, k to end [4 sts].

Row 12: p, cast off 2 at beg of row and p to end [2 sts].
Row 13: k2tog and cast off.

Left ear (make 1)
Cast on 5 sts in yellow
Rows 1–8: st st.
Row 9: k2tog at beg of row, k to end [4 sts]
Row 10: purl
Row 11: k2tog at beg of row, k to end [3 sts]
Row 12: purl and cast off.

Right ear (make 1)
Cast on 5 sts in yellow.
Rows 1–8: st st.
Row 9: k to last 2 sts and then k2tog [4 sts].
Row 10: purl.
Row 11: k to last 2 sts and then k2tog [3 sts].
Row 12: purl and cast off.

Tail (make 1)
Cast on 2 sts in yellow.
Row 1: inc each st [4 sts].
Row 2: purl, and change to brown.
Rows 3–4: *st st. Change to yellow.
Rows 5–6: st st. Change to brown*.
Rep from * to * until tail reaches desired length.
Cast off on the last purl row.

Making up
Fold the body in half and stitch up the back seam, leave neck open for stuffing. Fold the head in half and stitch from nose point down towards chin. Stitch the back of the head down to the neck. Stuff the head and pin it to the open neck edge of body before stitching the pieces together. Sew the feet to the bottom of the body, then sew the tail on at the back. Place the ears on either side of the head and sew on. Finish by sewing on two small beads for eyes.

Two Ulgarii hop past a waterfall on Glegg. These kangaroo-like aliens come in a bewildering variety of colours, textures and patterns, so go wild with your wool!

Verna

Materials:

2 balls 8-ply – 1 light brown and 1 variegated green

Small amount of purple yarn for mouths

Three pairs of beads for eyes

Polyester fibrefill

Sewing needle and black thread

Needles:

1 pair 3mm (UK 11; US 2) knitting needles

Instructions:

Face (make 3)

Cast on 3 sts in light brown.
Row 1: inc each st [6 sts].
Row 2: purl.
Row 3: inc each st [12 sts].
Rows 4–6: st st.
Row 7: k5, inc in each of next 2 sts, k5 [14 sts].
Rows 8–10: st st.
Row 11: k5, k2tog twice, k5 [12 sts].
Rows 12–14: st st.
Row 15: k2tog along row [6 sts].
Row 16: purl.
Row 17: k2tog along row [3 sts].
Row 18: purl and cast off.

Leaves (make 4)

Cast on 2 sts in variegated green.
Row 1: inc each st [4 sts].
Row 2: purl.
Row 3: inc each st [8 sts].
Row 4: purl.
Row 5: inc each st [16 sts].
Row 6: purl.
Row 7: cast off 3 sts at beg of row, k to end [13 sts].
Row 8: cast off 3 sts at beg of row, p to end [10 sts].
Row 9: cast on 3 sts at beg of row, k to end [13 sts].
Row 10: cast on 3 sts at beg of row, p to end [16 sts].
Row 11: cast off 5 sts at beg of row, k to end [11 sts].
Row 12: cast off 5 sts at beg of row, p to end [6 sts].
Rows 13–15: st st.
Row 16: p2tog [5 sts].
Row 17: knit and cast off.

Making up

Place two faces together and sew up side seam to the top. Place the third face between the two faces and stitch up each side seam to the top of the head. Stuff and sew the base shut. Needlesculpt each nose and sew on eyes, then embroider mouths. Stitch two leaves on top and two on the bottom.

The world of Xalliop is bathed in the gentle glow of two suns. The inhabitants enjoy basking so much that they take root and draw the food directly from sunlight, just like plants from our own planet. To keep them safe from harm, they have three faces on their bodies, so they can see all around themselves at once.

Ipris

Materials:

2 balls 8-ply – 1 turquoise and 1 cream

Small amount of pink yarn for mouth and cream yarn for antennae

2 beads for eyes

Polyester fibrefill

Sewing needle and black thread

Needles:

1 pair 3mm (UK 11; US 2) knitting needles

Instructions:

Body (make 2)

Cast on 12 sts in turquoise.
Rows 1–2: g st.
Row 3: k inc 1st st, k to end [13 sts].
Row 4: knit.
Row 5: k inc 1st st, k to end [14 sts].
Row 6: knit.
Rows 7–11: g st.
Row 12: k2tog at beg of row, k to end [13 sts].
Row 13: knit.
Row 14: k2tog at beg of row, k to end [12 sts].
Row 15: knit.
Row 16: k2tog at beg of row, k to end [11 sts].
Row 17: knit. Cast off.

Face (make 1)

Cast on 3 sts in cream.
Row 1: inc each st [6 sts].
Row 2: purl.
Row 3: inc each st [12 sts].
Row 4: purl.
Row 5: inc each st [24 sts].
Row 6: purl.
Row 7: k inc 1 each end [26 sts].
Row 8: purl.
Row 9: k inc 1 each end [28 sts].
Rows 10–14: st st.
Row 15: k2tog along row [14 sts].
Row 16: purl and cast off.

Legs (make 2)

Cast on 12 sts in turquoise.
Rows 1–5: g st.
Row 6: k2tog each end [10 sts].
Row 7: knit.
Row 8: k2tog each end [8 sts].
Row 9: knit.
Row 10: k2tog each end [6 sts].
Row 11: knit.
Row 12: k2tog three times and cast off.

Making up

Pin the body pieces together and sew them all the way around, leaving an opening at the neck. Stuff the body. Fold the head piece in half and sew it from the nose to the edge. Stuff the piece and stitch it into the neck opening of the body. Fold each leg in half and sew them along the seams. Stuff and stitch each into place on the sides of the body. Sew on beads for eyes, then make and attach two antennae and a tentacle (see page 7) for a tail. Embroider a nose with turquoise yarn, and make a mouth with pink yarn.

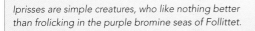

Iprisses are simple creatures, who like nothing better than frolicking in the purple bromine seas of Follittet.

Orbliona

Materials:

3 balls 8-ply – 1 lilac, 1 cream and 1 light purple

Small amount of turquoise yarn for the pupil
and purple yarn for antennae

Polyester fibrefill

Sewing needle and black thread

Needles:

1 pair 3mm (UK 11; US 2) knitting needles

Instructions:

Body (make 1)
Cast on 3 sts in lilac.
Row 1: inc each st [6 sts].
Row 2: purl.
Row 3: inc each st [12 sts].
Row 4: purl.
Row 5: inc each st [24 sts].
Row 6: purl.
Row 7: *k1, k inc 1*, rep from * to * to end of
row [36 sts].
Row 8: purl.
Row 9: *k1, k inc 1*, rep from * to * to end of
row [54 sts].
Rows 10–20: st st.
Row 21: *k1, k2tog*, rep from * to * to end of
row [36 sts].
Row 22: purl.
Row 23: *k1, k2tog*, rep from * to * to end of
row [24 sts].
Row 24: purl.
Row 25: k2tog along row [12 sts].
Row 26: purl.
Row 27: k2tog along row [6 sts].
Row 28: purl and cast off.

Eyeball (make 1)
Cast on 3 sts in cream.
Row 1: inc each st [6 sts].
Row 2: purl.
Row 3: inc each st [12 sts].
Rows 4–6: st st.
Row 7: k2tog along row [6 sts].

Row 8: purl.
Row 9: k2tog along row [3 sts].
Row 10: purl and cast off.

Eyelid (make 1)
Cast on 6 sts in light purple.
Row 1: purl.
Row 2: inc each st [12 sts].
Row 3: purl.
Row 4: k inc 1 each end [14 sts].
Rows 5–9: st st.
Row 10: k2tog each end [12 sts].
Row 11: purl.
Row 12: k2tog along row [6 sts].
Row 12: purl and cast off.

Making up
Fold the body in half and stitch down the
centre back seam from the top, leaving the
bottom open for stuffing. Stuff and stitch
closed. Repeat the process for the eyeball.
Wrap the eyelid around eyeball and stitch it in
place, then sew the eye to the body. Embroider
a pupil on to the eye with turquoise thread.
Make two antennae (see page 7) from purple
yarn and sew them in place on top of head.

Filled with lighter-than-air gasses and propelled by mind-power, Orbliones circle the rarified atmosphere of Porg at high speeds, zipping from place to place.

Bilpup

Materials:

2 balls 8-ply – 1 red and 1 cream

Small amount of fluffy yarn for neck ruffs, and purple yarn for neck details

4 beads for eyes

Polyester fibrefill

Sewing needle and black thread

Needles:

1 pair 3mm (UK 11; US 2) knitting needles

Instructions:

Body (make 1)

Cast on 10 sts in red.
Row 1: inc each st [20 sts].
Row 2: purl.
Row 3: inc 1 each end [22 sts].
Row 4: purl.
Row 5: inc 1 each end [24 sts].
Rows 6–10: st st.
Row 11: *k1, k inc 1* rep from * to * to end [36 sts].
Rows 12–20: st st.
Row 21: *k1, k2tog* rep from * to * to end [24 sts].
Row 22: purl.
Row 23: k2tog row [12 sts].
Row 24: k2tog row [6 sts].
Row 26: purl.
Row 27: k2tog row [3 sts].
Row 28: purl and cast off.

Head (make 2)

Cast on 3 sts in cream.
Row 1: inc each st [6 sts].
Row 2: purl.
Row 3: inc each st [12 sts].
Rows 4–8: st st.
Row 9: k inc each st [24 sts].
Row 10: purl.
Row 11: k8, inc each next 8 st, k8 [32 sts].
Rows 12–16: st st.
Row 17: k2tog row [16 sts].
Row 18: purl and cast off.

Neck (make 2)

Cast on 10 sts in purple.
Rows 1–2: st st. Bring in red.
Rows 3–4: st st. Change to purple.
Rows 5–6: st st. Change to red.
Rows 7–8: st st. Change to purple.
Rows 9–10: st st. Cast off.

Ears (make 4)

Cast on 6 sts in cream.
Row 1: knit.
Row 2: purl.
Row 3: k2tog each end [4 sts].
Row 4: purl.
Row 5: k2tog.
Row 6: purl and cast off.

Feet (make 4)

Cast on 3 sts in cream.
Row 1: inc each st [6 sts].
Row 2: purl.
Row 3: inc each st [12 sts].
Rows 4–7: st st.
Row 8: purl and cast off.

Making up

Fold the body in half and stitch up the centre back seam, leaving an opening at the top for stuffing. Stuff the body and stitch it shut. Roll the neck pieces up to form short fat rolls and stitch along the whole length of each. Once complete, stitch the necks on top of the body. Sew the head pieces from nose to neck opening and from the top of the back of the head to the neck opening. Stuff and stitch each to a neck. Stitch the ears in place and sew beads on for eyes. Sew each foot up at the back seam, stuff and stitch in place. Finally, weave a fancy yarn in and out of stitches at the bases of the necks for a fur ruff.

Drifting silently through the asteroid belt of Urxanda, Bilpuppies leap from rock to rock in search of seams of precious jewels on which to feed. Having two heads is a big advantage in avoiding a giant rock crashing into the asteroid on which you are standing!

Levinitus

Materials:

3 balls 8-ply – 1 green, 1 brown and 1 purple

Small amount of turquoise yarn for mouth

2 beads for eyes

Polyester fibrefill

Sewing needle and black thread

Needles:

1 pair 3mm (UK 11; US 2) knitting needles

Instructions:

Body (make 1)

Cast on 3 sts in green.
Row 1: inc each st [6 sts].
Row 2: purl.
Row 3: inc each st [12 sts].
Row 4: purl.
Row 5: inc each st [24 sts].
Row 6: purl.
Row 7: *k1, k inc 1* rep from * to * to end of row [36 sts].
Row 8: purl.
Row 9: *k1, k inc 1* rep from * to * to end of row [54 sts].
Rows 10–20: st st.
Row 21: *k1, k2tog* rep from * to * to end of row [36 sts].
Row 22: purl.
Row 23: *k1, k2tog* rep from * to * to end of row [24 sts].
Row 24: purl.
Row 25: k2tog along row [12 sts].
Row 26: purl.
Row 27: k2tog along row [6 sts].
Row 28: purl.
Row 29: k2tog along row [3 sts].
Row 30: purl. Cast off.

Head (make 1)

Cast on 3 sts in brown.
Row 1: inc each st [6 sts].
Row 2: purl.
Row 3: inc each st [12 sts].
Row 4: purl.
Row 5: inc each st [24 sts].
Row 6: purl.
Row 7: inc each st [48 sts].
Row 8: purl.
Rows 9–13: st st.

Row 14: k2tog along row [24 sts].
Row 15: purl.
Row 16: k2tog along row [12 sts].
Row 17: purl.
Row 18: k2tog along row [6 sts].
Row 19: purl. Cast off.

Ears (make 2)

Cast on 3 sts in purple.
Row 1: inc each st [6 sts].
Row 2: purl.
Row 3: inc each st [12 sts].
Rows 4–14: st st and cast off on last row.

Tentacles (make 7)

Cast on 1 st in brown.
Row 1: inc each st [2 sts].
Row 2: purl.
Row 3: inc each st [4 sts].
Rows 4–24: st st. Cast off on last row.

The Levinitii are a boastful species from Acquaskiot, and herald their arrival to new planets with their long, rambling and dirge-like poetry. Fortunately, their huge floppy ears, seven tentacles, general comical appearance and pompous attitudes means that most other aliens secretly find them hilarious, and always invite them round.

Making up

Fold the body in half and stitch from the top down the centre back seam, leaving a gap at the base open for stuffing. Stuff and stitch closed. Repeat for head. Sew head to body, aligning back seams. Stitch each tentacle up the length with the wrong sides together. Space them evenly around the body and sew them in place. Pin the ears to the top of head and sew them in place. Sew on two beads for eyes and embroider a simple mouth with turquoise thread. Make two antennae (see page 7) from green thread and sew them on top of the head. Needlesculpt the brow by taking a thread from near the eyes straight up to the top of the head and back down, pulling thread firmly but not too tight. Secure thread and neaten.

Pleshfur

Materials:

3 balls 8-ply – 1 cream, 1 yellow and 1 brown

Small amount of turquoise yarn for mouth, fancy yarn for frill and blue yarn for antennae

2 beads for eyes

Polyester fibrefill

Sewing needle and black thread

Needles:

1 pair 3mm (UK 11; US 2) knitting needles

Instructions:

Body and head (make 1)
Cast on 3 sts in cream.
Row 1: inc in each st [6 sts].
Row 2: purl.
Row 3: inc in each st [12 sts].
Row 4: purl.
Row 5: inc in each st [24 sts].
Row 6: purl. Bring in yellow.
Row 7: inc in each st [48 sts].
Change to cream.
Rows 8–9: st st. Change to yellow.
Rows 10–11: st st. Change to cream.
Rows 12–13: st st. Change to yellow.
Rows 14–15: st st. Change to cream.
Rows 16: Purl row. Change to yellow.
Row 17: k2tog along row [24 sts].
Row 18: purl.
Row 19: k2tog along row [12 sts].
Rows 20–22: st st.
Row 23: inc each st [24 sts].
Rows 24–32: st st. Change to cream.
Row 33: k2tog row [12 sts].
Row 34: purl.
Row 35: k2tog row [6 sts].
Row 36: purl.

Row 37: k2tog row [3 sts].
Row 38: purl. Cast off.

Face (make 1)
Cast on 3 sts in brown.
Row 1: inc each st [6 sts].
Row 2: purl.
Row 3: inc each st [12 sts].
Rows 4–6: st st.
Row 7: k5, inc in each of next 2 sts, k5 [14 sts].
Rows 8–10: st st.
Row 11: k5, k2tog twice, k5 [12 sts].
Rows 12–14: st st.
Row 15: k2tog along row [6 sts].
Row 16: purl.
Row 17: k2tog along row [3 sts].
Row 18: purl and cast off.

Legs (make 3)
Cast on 4 sts in brown.
Row 1: inc each st [8 sts].
Rows 2–17: st st. Cast off on the last row.

Arms (make 2)
Cast on 3 sts in brown.
Row 1: inc each st [6 sts].
Rows 2–15: st st.
Row 16: k2tog row [3 sts].
Row 17: purl and cast off.

Ears (make 2)
Cast on 3 sts in yellow.

Row 1: inc each st [6 sts].
Rows 2–8: st st. Cast off on the last row.

Making up
Fold the body in half, right sides together, and sew it up from the top of the head to the base of the body, leaving an opening large enough to push stuffing through. Stuff the body and stitch closed. Take the face and pin it to the middle of the front of the head. Stitch it on, stuffing as you go. Needlesculpt a nose. Sew the ears on top of the head, and attach two beads as eyes. Next, make two antennae (see page 7) from blue yarn and attach them to the top of the head. Sew the legs and arms up, with their wrong sides together. Stuff firmly. Place two of the legs at the front of the body and the third at the back like a tripod. Stitch in place. Place an arm on each shoulder and sew on. Weave a length of fancy yarn around the face to make a frill, and another one around the body beneath the armpits.

The eight-world system of Octori is home to the Pleshfuries, a fun-loving and gentle group of creatures.

Acknowledgments

A big thanks goes to my agent,
Isabel Atherton of Creative Authors;
Roz Dace, of Search Press;
Debbie Patterson for her beautiful
photography and last, but definitely
not least, my editor Edd Ralph for his
excellent help in putting these creatures
into a book (and putting up with their
many strange habits).

You are invited to visit the
author's website
www.fionamcdonald.com.au